2023

For Robyn, Wi...
Thank you
for The "Mike Connors
Calendar and the
great Picture.
It was so nice
Robyn to send us
the nice gifts.
Always, Mak

Always,
Mark Keys

My
BEST
DAY

ACTORS I

a collection of best day responses from actors, directors,
singers, and others in the entertainment industry

MARK KEYS

H-949-645-8109 *Mark, Laurie & Family*
C-949-531-1373 *Laurie's Cell #*

M K
C E
C Y
O S
O
L

PRESS

Dedicated to one of my heroes: Kirk Douglas. I met him in Palm Desert at the Frank Sinatra Celebrity Golf and again at Cedar Sinai. He was a true-life Spartacus

INTRODUCTION

In May 1991, I injured my back while working and was placed on permanent disability. Prior to my first back surgery, I had my photo taken with Magic Johnson of the Los Angeles Lakers. Later, Blain Skinner, a friend of mine, was able to get Magic to autograph the snapshot. It made my day.

As a hobby, I began writing to other celebrities asking for autographed photos. Their positive responses amazed me. One weekend while in Palm Springs, California, I met Nat Kipner, an entrepreneur, who suggested I expand my hobby to include famous people from all walks of life. This idea was a godsend. During the next several years, while incapacitated with several more back surgeries and an ankle reconstruction, I collected even more autographs.

One day while out walking, I noticed the magnificent beauty of the simple blue sky. Upon returning home, I thought about what a good day it was, despite my back problems. I felt great! Then it struck me: I wondered what all those people I had been receiving autographs from felt was their "best day."

I began writing letters asking that question. Joey Bishop was the first to reply, and that's how it all began.

McCool Keys Press
5308 Neptune
Newport Beach, CA 92663

Individual Sales, this book is available through most bookstores or can be ordered directly from McCool Keys Press at the address above.

Quantity Sales. Special discounts are available on quantity purchases by corporations, associations, and others. For details, contact the "Special Sales Department" at the publisher's address above.

Printed in the United States of America.

Cover design: Escher Creative eschercreative@sbcglobal.net
949-400-5987

Library of Congress Cataloging-in-Publication Data is available from the publisher.

ISBN 978-0-9897878-6-4

ACKNOWLEDGEMENTS:

Dedicated in the memory David "Bucko" Shaw, who always made me laugh, & who I miss everyday

Thank you to all those who were supportive and encouraging to my project: Rick John, Mike Wilsey and family, John Hamilton and Diane, Michael Dante, Kobe Bryant, Jack Lemmon, Dean Martin- his daughter Deana Martin & John Griffeth, Tony Curtis, James MacArthur, Kirk & Ann Douglas, Ted McGinley, Don Rickles, and Bob Newhart. Cassavete Winstead, The McCarthy Family, Frank Venclick & his parents Frank & Betty, Fred Howser Jim & Cathie Helfrich, Mary Claire Helfrich and the entire Helfrich Family, Steve Foley, Frank & Connie Clark, Chris & Jane Clark and boys, Dan & Sheila Rogers, Joe Rodgers and family, Jon Sweek, Brad Leggett, Janet Curci, Heather Hendrickson and her mom; Marilyn, Mark & Leslie Louvier, Laurie Weddington-Tagg, Lora Mulligan, Gordon Adams & Family, Gene & Barb Kraus, Chet & Varina McCabe, Pat Millican, My "brothers" Fraser & Chris Keys, Steve Kalatschan, Kevin Doody, Dave Roum, Chris Rock, Sports Writer Sam Farmer, Anadan Barragan, Jon & Jane Arnett, Fred & Natalie Lynn, Steve Virgen, Randy & Gaye McIlwain, Barry & Sheila Wood, Dan & Michelle Parke, Mike & Dave Thompson, The Hanley Brothers, Burt Sirota, Nigel & Michelle Kent, Ted & Christine. As always, my mom, Virginia and my mother-in-law, Glenell. A big thank you to Aunt Joan Parker, your help is immeasurable. Thank you Erik Escher for the cover and banner ads

Thank you TCM, Robert Osborne and Ben Mankiewicz

Thank you to all of my doctors over the years: Gausewitz, Kimberly Safman & Naomi Porter, Rhie, Gerken, Bae, Hunt, Quist, O'Carroll & Gladys Mendoza, Carlson & Katie, Bruss, Yaru – Julia & Pearl, Dobkin, Nassif, Ting, Gordon, Shukla, Stringer, Wynn, Ali Sheets, Feinberg, Newman, Cleereman.

Thank you to my wife Laurie. She has been there for me always, especially after I got hurt and has been involved with my project every step of the way. To my wonderful daughters, Megan & Page— I love you with all of my heart.

Also by Mark Keys

SERIES

AS SEEN ON

https://www.espn.com/video/clip/_/id/11924279

 Mybestday_MK   mybestdaybyMarkKeys   markkeys0405

McCool Keys Press - Newport Beach

FORWARD

I met Mark Keys at the Hollywood Show in Los Angeles, California. He came to my table to buy my autobiography, *Michael Dante-From Hollywood To Michael Dante Way*. We got acquainted as I autographed a copy to him and he shared with me about a book he was writing entitled, *My Best Day*. I was immediately attracted to the fact that it was a collection of 'best day remembrances of actors, directors, musicians, entertainers and writers from movies and television.' Mark mentioned it as a hobby; writing to two celebrities asking for autographed photos and their responses to the question, "What is your best day?" He received back positive, funny and uplifting comments.

It all began when Mark was unable to work and was recuperating from several surgeries. One day while walking, it struck him that all those people he had been receiving autographs from, shared what had been their 'best day.' It was quite an impressive list of names and answers from many talented people in the entertainment industry. The fact that, to help ease his pain, he had found something special to take his mind off his discomfort was remarkable. Mark had created something that gave him a reason to carry on every day. He rose above it all by living a creative life. I admired his attitude, his sincere desire to learn about other people's 'best day' and then share their answers with everyone through the writing of this book.

When he asked me if I would do an interview with him about my 'best day,' I was happy to answer, but it took me a while to express it because I have been truly blessed with so many good days in my life. Finally, the answer came, and I was more than happy to have shared it with Mark and you, his readers.

I hope you enjoy Mark's book, *My Best Day*, as much as I do and it will give you food for thought when asked the question, "What is your best day?"

-MICHAEL DANTE
Award Winning Actor, Award Winning Author

Any day above ground is a great day to me!

-TERI GARR

Actress; Tootsie, Young Frankenstein, Mr. Mom, Friends

My "best day" was the day I received your invitation to share a personal thought with response to "what was your best day?" It made me start thinking and realizing what a fortunate person I am. I've had so many "best days" that have meant so much to me. Just thinking through so many of those days and what the memories brought me, and meant to me, filled my day with happiness and gratitude. What wonderful meaningful memories I had that day about family and friends and work and play. I laughed and I cried. It was a day like no other. Thanks for asking, boy did you make my day.

-ARTHUR HILLER

Actor; Love Story, Plaza Suite, The Out-of-Towners

Atticus Finch, getting that role was my lucky day! When Alan Pacula & Bob Mulligan sent me the book, saying I think this is something you are going to like. I sat up all night reading the book, and I could hardly wait to call them. I wanted to call them at 3:00 in the morning to say, "if you want me, I'm your boy." I never had a moments regret. It was a blessing and a gift from Harper Lee.

-GREGORY PECK

Actor; To Kill A Mockingbird, Roman Holiday, Moby Dick. Spell Bound

Each day that I wake up becomes my best!

-MIKE CONNERS

Actor; Sudden Fear, Good Sam, The Ten Commandments, Tightrope! Mannix

One of my best days was being hired to emcee TCM, I get to watch the films I love and interview actors I enjoy watching. One of my favorite movies is "Laura", because Gene Tierney is one of my favorite actresses.

-ROBERT OSBORNE

TCM Host, Desilu Playhouse, The Californian

The day I arrived in New York, in 1946, on my way to Hollywood MGM. My contract was signed and sealed, and I was about to appear in the Hucksters with Clark Gable… It was more exciting to me making my Hollywood debut with such a big star, at the tender age of 25!

-DEBORAH KERR
Actress; The Hucksters, King Solomon's Mines, An Affair to Remember, From Here to Eternity

My best day was March 5, 1948 the day I married Anne Jackson. We have been married for over sixty years and still making it work.

-ELI WALLACH

Actor; Baby Doll, The Good, Bad and the Ugly, The Magnificent Seven, The Misfits, Mystic River

My best day was October 18th, 2010 when my husband, Eli Wallach, received the "Alumni Finley Award" at City College of New York.

-ANNE JACKSON
Actress; The Bell Jar, The Shinning, The Secret Life of an American Wife

EVERY DAY is my BEST DAY! And I hope your days are the same.

-SIDNEY SHELDON

Writer & Producer, Patty Duke Show, Other Side of Midnight, I Dream of Jeannie, Rage of Angels

The first response that comes to mind when you ask me about my best day is the morning I got to meet and interview Katharine Hepburn at her brownstone apartment in New York City. She couldn't have been more forthcoming, and we seemed to hit it off right away. I had seen a mutual friend a few days earlier so that was my ice breaker and it seemed to work. While the crew was setting up our cameras, we chatted, and when we moved into position to do the "official" interview, we simply kept it up. She's a great interview because she is so direct and opinionated. It doesn't hurt that she leads a fascinating life. When our allotted time was over, I didn't want to leave…and in fact, I didn't, until every bit of equipment was packed up and there was no way to linger another minute. I'll never forget that day.

-LEONARD MALTIN
Movie Critic/Author; Entertainment Tonight

I was having one of my best days in Palm Springs attending our friend Barbara Sinatra's fundraiser for her center for abused children, when Mark Keys asked me to send him a description of my "best day."

I gave it a lot of thought and realized that I am lucky to have had so many best days that I am now going to write my own damn book. Like Pearl Baily said, "If I can't see it, I'm going to sit on it, because I ain't giving nothin' away."

So, Mark, you go buy my book and I'll buy yours and that way we'll both have another "best day."

-GEORGE SCHLATTER

Writer/Producer; Get Bruce, Norman, is that You? Laugh-in, American Comedy Awards

Everyday!

GEORGE KENNEDY
Actor; Cool Hand Luke, The Eiger Sanction, Airport, In Harm's Way

The first-time kissing John Wayne in Rio Bravo!

-ANGIE DICKINSON

Actress; Rio Bravo, Sabrina, Oceans 11, Hollywood Wives, Police Woman

In 1963, I won the most valuable player award while pitching softball for the Negro Actors Guild in the Broadway show *League*.

-GEORCE C. SCOTT

Actor/Director; Patton, Dr. Strangelove, The Day of the Dolphin, Anatomy of a Murder, Taps

I have had many best days in my career…one of my favorites is:

I guest-starred in Desilu Playhouse with Rory Calhoun and Janice Rule in a true story based on the life of boxer Joey Barnum, "The Killer Instinct." Having done a terrific job playing a boxer, the very next day I was offered *two* contracts: Twentieth Century Fox, one picture a year for five years beginning with "Seven Thieves" co-starring Rod Steiger, Edward G. Robinson, and Joan Collins. The second contract was with Desilu Productions starring in "The Untouchables" with Robert Stack for 13 episodes, rotating with him, one week on and one week off. I wanted to do films, not television, so I chose the picture deal with Twentieth Century Fox. It was one of my best decisions and days…and the rest is history!

-MICHAEL DANTE
Actor; Winter Hawk, The Naked Kiss. Fort Dobbs, Apache Rifles, Harlow

I've had many highlights in my life-both personally and professionally. I believe each day is my Best Day. Like the saying "today is a gift, that is why it is called the present'. That is how I live my life.

-RYAN O'NEAL
Actor; Paper Moon, Love Story, Peyton Place, What's up Doc?

I have had so many favorite days, but I can tell you that my favorite film was "The Rainmaker"

-EARL HOLLIMAN

Actor; The Gunfight at the O K Corral, The Sons of Katie Elder, Sharkey's Machine, The Rainmaker, Police Woman

Becoming a dad when Jack was born was my Best Day ever. But, my Best Day in my career was when I was discovered. I was living out of my van in Maui and was a waiter at "Bubba Gump Shrimp". It actually was the time of my life- I made good money & enjoyed the beach life. I was serving a female producer who said I was cute, and asked if I was an actor? I said "yes, you should put me in a movie". (I was "acting that I was an actor, because at that point I was not an actor") Four days later I was in LA for a screen test and I never went back.

-CHRIS PRATT

Actor; Jurassic World, Guardians of the Galaxy, Parks and Recreation, Magnificent Seven

When I was on the Carol Burnett show was always a best day, it was so much fun. All we did was laugh and have fun.

-HARVEY KORMAN

Actor; The April Fools, Blazing Saddles, High Anxiety, Trial of the Pink Panther, The Tim Conway Show

Being with my lovely wife, Shera, and family, painting and getting the great character of Columbo—all best days in my life.

-PETER FALK

Actor, The Great Race, The Brinks Job, Robin and the 7 Hoods, Columbo

Every day is a Best Day and being with my beautiful family!

-SIDNEY POITIER

Actor; Blackboard Jungle, Lilies of the Field, The defiant Ones, Porgy and Bess, A Raisin in the Sun, Guess Who's Coming to Dinner

There is no other possibility for my best days that the day Helen Hayes MacArthur and Charles MacArthur decided to adopt me. It made my life what it has been. Without them I have no idea where I would be. Perhaps, in another good place…perhaps not. I am only grateful that I never knew the other option!

JAMES MacARTHUR

Actor; Hawaii 5-0, Swiss Family Robinson, Kidnapped, Spencer's Mountain

The Best Day for me was the day I met my wife Pamela

-HARRY BELAFONTE

Singer; "Banana Boat Song", "Island in the Sun", "Jump in Line" Actor;
Tonight with Belafonte, Island in the Sun, Uptown Saturday Night, Bobby,
BlacKkKlansman

Every day is my best day.

-LLOYD BRIDGES

Actor; High Noon, Little Big Horn, Airplane!, Sea Hunt

My Best Day? Tomorrow.

-JAMES GREGORY

Actor; Naked City, The Manchurian Candidate, Barney Miller

There are so many best days to choose from, but one best day was filming "Big" with Tom Hanks, it was pure joy. The piano scene was so much fun.

-ROBERT LOGGIA

Actor; Scarface, Prizzi's Honor, Gladiator, Independence Day, Big

I've been blessed with so many "best days" that I cannot choose a favorite. Even better—each new morning brings that possibility of yet another "best".

-RICHARD ERDMAN

Actor / Director, Nobody Lives Forever, The San Francisco Story, Stalag 17, The Men

Getting a star on the Hollywood Walk of Fame is truly an honor, and absolutely My Best Day in acting. The TV series Wonder Woman gave birth to my career as a superhero and

feminist icon. It seems impossible, but I have been in the entertainment industry for more than 50 years. Acting, singing, and entertainment and I have loved it all.

I think back to those early years when I faced the struggles and challenges that a young actor confronts, including the inevitable rejections and bad reviews, those fade away. I love this business, all of it. I love the creative process, love the work, love the performing. But, my fondest memories about this career are the wonderful people that I have met.

-LYNDA CARTER
Actress; Wonder Woman, Sky High, The Last Song, Super Girl

Every day I consider a best day. Too difficult to pick just one. I just thank God for all my blessings.

-JULIA MEADE

Actress; Pillow Talk, Tammy Tell Me True, My First Love, Presumed Innocent

My best day was September 21, 1958 when I married Toby. Except I never realized it was until she passed away June 21, 2001. It was forty-three years of best days. My three boys understand this and love me even though they know they're in second place.

-JED ALLAN

Actor; Days of our Lives, Santa Barbara, Beverly Hills 90210, The Bay

Wow! As the years encroach upon my memories, I think of all the loving, sharing, and laughing in a sweeping continuum so that one day does not stick out as better than many others…

My children's births, my happy youthful exuberance and prolonged periods without pain are among those I enjoyed immensely…oh, yes, there was another…the day Nixon died. Mean as that sounds, it was much meaner to be on his enemies list.

-AVERY SCHREIBER

Actor / Comedian; My Mother the Car, Robin Hood: Men in Tights

My best day is every day, because I'm in charge-I plan it-I fix it-I enjoy it always.

-RIP TORN

Comedian/ Actor; King of Kings, The Presidents Plane is Missing, Defending your Life, Men in Black

After much reflection, the obvious banner days of four healthy children brought into this world...I feel the best day was when film icon Robert Redford invited me to play legendary *Twenty-One* TV host, Jack Berry in his acclaimed film, Quiz Show. What made it so special was he did that with just a look into my eyes, artist to artist, without an audition—and he knew I could do it. It remained a high point in my filmography.

-CHRIS MC DONALD

Quiz Show, Spy Kids, Happy Gilmore, Thelma & Louise

My best day was when I was hired for "Days" and Bold and Beautiful.

-JOSEPH MASCOLO

Actor, Days of Our Lives, Bold and the Beautiful, Sharkey's Machine, Heat

Today is my best day! I have all of the yesterdays to remember and all the tomorrows to look forward to.

-LLOYD BOCHNER

Actor, Dynasty, Twilight Zone, The Detective, Tony Rome

I remember I was 14 years old and my SAG card came in the mail after I did a promo for the MTV movie "my Super Sweet 16". It was the Best Day of my entire life because it meant I was officially a professional actor which put me with all other great actors.

-JENNIFER LAWRENCE

Actress; The Hunger Games, X-Men, Silver Lining Playbook, American Hustle

I've had a lot of good ones, a number of bad ones, and a bunch in between. It is also true that I look to my days right now and in the future for some degree of joy and satisfaction. I guess I do dwell much on the past.

-LEN LESSER

Actor, Seinfeld, Outlaw Josey Wales, Some Came Running, Kelly's Hero's

Every day is my best day!

-JERRY MATHERS

Actor; Leave it to Beaver, My Three Sons, The Girl, the Gold Watch and Dynamite

Best/Worst day for me was the last day of "The Leave it to Beaver" show. I had so much fun and was blessed with so many great friends it was hard to leave. That show was the best.

-TONY DOW
Actor; The Eleventh Hour, Adam-12, Back to the Beach, Dickie Roberts; Child Star

Today is definitely my best day!

-BARBARA BILLINGSLEY

Actress; Leave it to Beaver, The Bad and the Beautiful, Prejudice

Every day is my best day and each day gets better and better. What you think is the reason for having great days. The two most memorable "best days" were:

June 22, 1976 when my daughter Taylor Van was born and her dad Bobby Van was announcing the birth on his morning show on NBC, and February 10, 1986 when my son Mick Levoff was born. I don't think it gets better than that.

-ELAINE JOYCE

Actress; Love Boat, Beverly Hills 90210, City of Angels

I know a lot of people were surprised when Ashton and I started dating. But, one day, our friendship simply turned into something more.

All of a sudden, it wasn't the same. And I was really proud of myself for acknowledging that. The Best Day of my life so far was the proposal. I cried. I was a mess. Not to discredit any relationships in my past, but this relationship is different. Giving birth to our daughter Wyatt and son Demitri comes in right behind the proposal, which lead to our children. I am blessed.

-MILA KUNIS
Actress; Black Swan, The Book of Eli, Oz the Great and Powerful, Bad Moms, That 70s Show

There is no way I could pick a "best" or a "worst". I have been blessed with so many great days and events that each, although different, is special. And none of them would mean as much if not contrasted with some dismal dark days. Often people ask me to choose a favorite role, or picture and my usual flip answer is "the next one."

In the same light I have been asked WHO INSPIRED ME MOST and again there are so many equal choices. I have decided that, for me, life is a composite and I couldn't appreciate something today if I hadn't experienced something earlier to give it perspective. Nor could a joy today be as great were it not contrasted with a soul-shaking sorrow.

-DABBS GREER

Actor; The Unknown Man, Affair with a Stranger, The Green Mile, Rockford Files, Cannon

My best day? Easy! December 25, 2005. The birth of Christ and the day I found out my wife, Sam, was pregnant with our first child.

-KEVIN SORBO

Actor; Kull the Conqueror, Andromeda, Soul Surfer, Confessions of a Prodigal Son, Hercules

The day I auditioned for the movie, *From Here to Eternity*. My career was at an all-time low, and I had to pull strings to get an audition. I knew I was born to play Maggio. I did the "bar scene" and improvised by picking up olives to use as dice to roll "snake eyes" to impress the director. I got the role and went on to win an Oscar for Best Supporting Actor as Maggio.

-FRANK SINATRA as told by Tom Dreesen

Actor/Singer, The Man with the Golden Arm, Oceans 11, Suddenly, Von Ryan's Express

My best day is being with family and friends.

-MAUREEN MC CORMICK

Actress / Singer, The Brady Bunch, The Idol Maker, Dogtown

While playing with my brother, Les Brown's Band of Renown, at the Hollywood Palladium in October 1943, I was introduced to a beautiful 14-year-old girl at the afternoon dance we played on Sundays. After many years later, we started to date. We were married on April 29, 1957. I'm happy to say, comes that day in 2007, we will celebrate our 50th Wedding anniversary.

-CLYDE "STUMPY" BROWN
Bass Trombonist and vocalist with Les Brown

October 6, 1993—I was shooting Picket Fences at Twentieth Century Fox (it's always a good day when an actor is working). But it turned into my best day when Peggy and I met at the commissary-we wed the following May- my Irish Colleen has made my life complete.

-JAMES CALLAHAN

Actor; The Detective, Lady Sings the Blues, M*A*S*H, Charles in Charge

My Best day? When I was fourteen and discovered acting. Every day has been a best day ever since.

-GENA ROWLANDS

Actress; Lonely are the Brave, Gloria, The Notebook, A Women Under the Influence

I have to say that my best day was the opening night of *Zoot Suit* at Mark Taper Forum in Los Angeles.

-EDWARD JAMES OLMOS

Actor; Miami Vice, Stand and Deliver, Blade Runner

I was in the Navy in World War II after two years in the South Pacific when our ship sailed under the Golden Gate Bridge in San Francisco—officers and crew broke down and cried. That was my best day.

-LARRY STORCH

Actor; Sex and the Single Girl, The Great Race, Airport 1975, S.O.B., F-Troop

The best days of my life (two) were when I gave birth to my children.

-BLYTHE DANNER

Actress; Huff, 1776, Meet the Parents, Meet the Fockers

We live by hope for tomorrow. So, I guess my best day is yet to come. It's something to always look forward to- "look-look-look to the rainbow."

-NORMAN JEWISON
Director, In the Heat of the Night, Cincinnati Kid, The Thomas Crown Affair, And Justice for all

I love to sing, and perform—each day I can do it is a best day. Like today, here we are the Frank Sinatra Golf Tournament, getting to have the Keys family as my audience in the main ballroom while I rehearse for the gala tonight. I am so blessed.

-LOU RAWLS

Singer

The day I was born, (November 20, 1908!) on my father's birthday.

-ALISTAIR COOKE

Journalist & Broadcaster; Masterpiece Theater, Three Faces of Eve, America:A Personal History of the United States

I just cannot answer your question. My lifetime honestly gives me a best day every day, nearly every week.

-BING RUSSELL

Actor; Durango, Gun Fight of the OK Corral, The Magnificent Seven, Ride a Violent Mile,

I got goose bumps peering through the small triangular window onto the craggy surface of the moon. The Lunar Modules Descent was perfect. Nearly hyperventilating with excitement, I pushed off the last rung of the ladder, and dropping gently onto the powdery-wait a minute-that wasn't me...that was an astronaut, you know, uh, what's his name...oh well. Hey, I'll bet that was his best day though.

-BRYAN CRANSTON

Actor; Saving Private Ryan, Drive, Trumbo, Malcom in the Middle, Breaking Bad

My best day was the last day of filming in Death Valley, on *Three Godfathers* in July 1948. The reason was that it was my best day was because John Ford was very, very hard on me, all through the filming of *Three Godfathers*.

-HARRY CAREY JR

Actor; Red River, Three Godfathers, She wore a Yellow Ribbon, Searchers, Tombstone

My Best Day is today, and my next best day is tomorrow, and every day is my "Best Day."

-LARRY HAGMAN

Actor; Harry and Tonto, Nixon, Primary Colors, Dallas, I Dream of Jeannie

Any day is a best day…I love my life, family, and acting. There have been too many to choose.

-JEFF GARLIN

Actor; Sleep Over, Fun with Dick and Jane, Toy Story 3, Cars 2, Curb Your Enthusiasm

My best day was January 21, 1981, when I saw my best friend, Ronald Reagan, sworn in as president of the United States in Washington, He appointed me to his advisory board with offices in the OEB at the White House.

Another "Best Day" was the first time I saw the title on the screen "produced by A.C. Lyles." My career at Paramount had advanced from office boy for Adolph Zucker, founder of Paramount, to producer.

Another best day was when I celebrated my eightieth birthday and at the same time my seventieth anniversary with Paramount. It's a short resume: "1928-2000: Paramount."

-A.C. LYLES

Producer; Law of the Lawless, Young and The Brave, Red Tomahawk

My Best Day is always the next day.

-ANDREW V. MC LAGLEN

Director, Chisum, McLintock!, Shenandoah, The Way West, Bandolero!

My Best Day was being on M*A*S*H.

-WAYNE ROGERS

Actor; Cool Hand Luke, The Killing Time, Love Lies Bleeding, House Calls,
*M*A*S*H*

My Best Day was the summer of '63. Living in our first home which had a half acre of hillside. My wife had gone to the obstetrician being with our soon-to-be first born. I was clearing brush on the slope with a big guy from North Carolina and Howard, his wino helper. All of a sudden, I see our car come up the water tank road which bottomed our property. I became fearful that something had gone wrong at the doctors. Then I relaxed, knowing that she wouldn't be driving like a bat out of hell if she weren't in a good mood. She got out of the car and imperiously ordered me to come down the slope to her. I snarled "what for?" and she demanded my descent, Halfway down I stopped, looked at her and said "Really?" and she smiled and nodded yes. I leaped for joy and guessed she'd found out we were having twins. What a nice day, I shouted to the Carolinian, "Bill, she's having twins!", and he congratulated me. Then, not wanting to slight the wino, I said, "Howard, she's having twins." And he responded, "Yeah. I am a twin." I clutched my heart and fought to keep from asking, what does your brother do?"

-ED ASNER

Actor; UP, ELF, Mary Tyler Moore Show, Lou Grant, Roots,
Rich Man, Poor Man,

My Best Day? Today!

-BETTY WHITE

Actress; Hot in Cleveland, Golden Girls, Mary Tyler Moore Show, The Proposal

Aside from my three children being born…the day World War II ended. I was in Iwo Jima and hadn't seen my wife for sixteen months.

-CARL REINER

Actor/Director, It's a Mad, Mad, Mad World, The Dick Van Dyke Show, The Jerk, 2000-Year-Old Man,

When I married John Griffeth

-DEANA MARTIN
Author/Singer/Actress; Young Billy Love, Strangers at Sunset

Today is my Best Day.

-DEAN MARTIN

Actor/Singer; Ocean's 11, Rio Bravo, 5 Card Stud, Dean Martin Roasts, Dean Martin Variety Hour

Getting the go-ahead for *Damn Yankees,* my first trip to Broadway…and the days ever since.

-JERRY LEWIS

Actor/Director/Writer/Producer; The Nutty Professor, Cinderfella, MS Labor Day Telethon

Every day I am here is a best day, but some of my best days was working on films; especially with Jack Lemmon, being with family and starting the Shiloh Horse Rescue Ranch with my wife, Jill.

-TONY CURTIS

Actor / Painter; Spartacus, Some Like it Hot, Defiant Ones, The Great Race

I have had two best days: the birth of my daughter, Carrie, and the birth of my son, Todd. They have been my greatest source of happiness throughout the years and I thank the good Lord every day for the blessings He has bestowed on me, through my children.

An added bonus (and very definite treat!) has been the added blessing of Carrie's baby, my granddaughter, Billie Catherine, who warms my heart and calls me "Sparkle"! She's darling and I love her with all my heart!.

-DEBBIE REYNOLDS

Actor/Singer; Singing in the Rain, Tammy and the Bachelor, How the West was Won, Unsinkable Molly Brown, Halloweentown

The day I married my wife-fifty-six years ago January 14, 1941

-JOEY BISHOP

Actor / Host; Oceans 11, Joey Bishop Show

I have had five best days, each at the birth of a child, the last birth being twins. But the kind of day to which you must have referenced is the day I read the following bit of philosophy: "At the moment of commitment the entire universe conspires to assure your success."

-NORMAN LEAR

Writer; All in the Family, The Jefferson's, Maude, One Day at a Time,

The day I started The Lone Ranger TV shows.

-CLAYTON MOORE

Actor; Kit Carson, Tuxedo Junction, Bandits of El Dorado, Lone Ranger, The Ghost of Zorro

…The day my baby girl was born, because I had stated that I wanted a girl child and went to work with charts and thermometers to get her. She was born on the morning of September 9, 1971.

-MORGAN FREEMAN

Actor; Driving Miss Daisy, Bruce Almighty, The Shawshank Redemption, The Unforgiven, Invictus, Million Dollar Baby

The day Christian Slater's interview in People magazine came out. Christian, when asked…to choose a role model…he chose me. Since I'm very close to Christian, that meant a lot to me. That same night Charles Durning and Peter Falk were at a play reading that I put together. I overheard my name being mentioned and Peter saying, "That Dan is a hell of an actor", Charles replied, "and a good guy." Love and respect from my peers, what more could I ask for in one day?

-DAN LAURIA

Actor; Stake Out, Independence Day, Prison of Secrets, The Wonder Years, The Spirit, Sullivan & Sons

With the exception of the birth of my kids, I have not had a Best Day yet. I keep looking forward to tomorrow, so each day can be a Best Day.

-JOEY LAWRENCE

Actor; Oliver & Company, Blossom, Brotherly Love, Melissa & Joey, CSI – NY, Hawaii 50, Dancing with the Stars

My best day? I've had so many. Playing the Palace on Broadway in vaudeville with my sister Velma in 1930 was certainly one. Opening in Flying Colors, a Broadway show, with Velma was another. Winning the Trans Pac in my catamaran was certainly a best day. But, thinking back over the years, reviewing the paths I traveled, and where I am today, my best day was the day I married Dorothy.

-BUDDY EBSEN

Actor; Yellow Jacket, Silver City Bonanza, Beverly Hillbillies, Barnaby Jones, Davy Crockett

My Best Day- I wake up feeling grateful. I feel grateful all day long.

I go to sleep saying Thank you, Thank You.

-ALLEY MILLS
Actress; The Associates, The Wonder Years, Dr. Quinn, Medicine Woman, The Bold and the Beautiful,

Every day I wake up and read the obituary. If I am not in it, I go about my business. That makes each day, a Best Day!

-ORSON BEAN
Actor; Being John Malkovich, To Tell the Truth, Mary Hartman, Mary Hartman; Dr Quinn, Medicine Woman, Broadway's Will Success Spoil Rock Hunter

My best day is receiving this letter from you (Mark Keys)

-BILL DAILY

Actor/Director; The Barefoot Executive, Murder at the Mardi Gras, Bob Newhart Show, I Dream of Jeannie

Every day has the best day potential.

-BONNIE HUNT

*Actress; Rain Man, The Green Mile, Jerry Maguire, Cheaper by the Dozen,
The Bonnie Hunt Show*

The eve of the Riverside 500 in 1964. Seated at the head of the pre-race dinner was my soulmate, Shelby Grant-she was Queen of the Riverside 500. The moment I laid eyes on her I was, as the Italians say, "thunderstruck." We are approaching our thirtieth anniversary.

-CHAD EVERETT

Actor; Johnny Tiger, Mulholland Drive, Medical Center, Ironside

When my children were born.

-JACK KLUGMAN
Actor; 12 Angry Men, The Detective, Two-Minute Warning, Odd Couple, Quincy M. E.

The day my national actor's theater finally came into being in 1991 – it was truly the realization of my dreams.

-TONY RANDALL
Actor; Will Success Spoil Rock Hunter? Pillow Talk, Lover Come Back, Arsenic and Old Lace, The Tony Randall Show, The Odd Couple

Any day I don't have a root canal is a good day.

-PHYLLIS DILLER

*Comedian/Actress; Boy, Did I Get a Wrong Number, A Pleasure Doing
Business, A Bugs Life, Phyllis Diller Show*

When I first headlined at the Flamingo Hotel in Las Vegas. After doing primarily comedy in my act for years I decided to add a dramatic talk doing the final scene in Camelot as Richard Burton! I was given a standing ovation, stopped my own show, I couldn't have been more thrilled. For one brief moment I had my best day.

-FRANK GORSHIN

Actor/Impressionist, "The Riddler" in Batman TV Series, Warlock, The Great Imposter, The George Raft Story

My best day is today.

-WALTER MATTHAU

Actor; Grumpy Old Men, The Odd Couple, The Fortune Cookie, Taking of Pellham One, Two, Three

Really haven't had a bad day. My best day is yet to come, and I
enjoy looking and living for it every day, honest!

-HUGH O'BRIAN
Actor; Wyatt Earp, The Shootist, "Hugh O'Brian Youth Leadership Council"

When I met Frank!

-BARBARA SINATRA
Model/Philanthropist

When I sold my book for a thrilling $1,910 and had been promised a first printing of 500 copies. Life had never been so sweet. Second to the birth of my daughter, it was the best day of my life.

-J.K. ROWLING

Author, Harry Potter and the Sorcerer's Stone, Harry Potter Series

When you live to be 90+... It's almost impossible to single out one particular best day... Oh, of course today I met Betty, my wife of 62 years, opening night at the Pasadena Playhouse, my first screen test... And when I got the contract... Maybe the best day of all was Christmas Eve when my brother and I hid on the upstairs landing and watched my dad bring a flexible Flyer sled into the house... What a Christmas that was – snow and everything!

Actually, I loved my work so that each day there was a great, great pleasure on set.

Another Best Day was my 90th birthday party. My four daughters were there, the grandchildren and great-grandchildren, plus Margaret O'Brien, Jane Wyatt, Roddy McDowall, Elinore Donahue and Billy Grey. I also received a lovely tribute letter from President Clinton.

-ROBERT YOUNG
Actor; Hell Below, Spitfire, The Three Wise Guys, Northwest Passage, Marcus Welby, M.D., Father Knows Best

The best? I guess the one film of mine with the fewest mistakes:
The Apartment.

-BILLY WILDER
Screenwriter/ Director/ Producer, Some Like It Hot, The Apartment, Stalag 17

My Best Day? I've had so many, I'm the luckiest guy alive. I guess the best day was the day I was born when the good Lord handed me the gift of this wonderful life.

-ROBERT STACK

Actor; My Outlaw Brother, The Tarnished Angels, Airplane!
Uncommon Valor, The Untouchables,

Christmas, and all that it means!

-JUNE ALLYSON
Actress; The Three Musketeers, Little Women, Glenn Miller Story, Executive Suite, My Man Godfrey

The birth of my babies, my wedding day/days, my discovery, my first movie… My children being my friends.

-JANET LEIGH

Actress / Dancer; Touch of Evil, Bye, Bye Birdie, Houdini, Psycho, The Manchurian Candidate

My years with Burns and Allen, my many seasons with Jack Benny, the fun I had with Fred McMurray on My Three Sons, my 22 years with Johnny Carson, the very pleasant relationship I am having now with Jay Leno. Let's just say I've had a lot of good times

-FRED DE CORDOVA

Director/Producer, Burns and Allen, the Tonight Show

Career-best day: I auditioned for *"Call me Mister"* in 1946 and I got the job. Personally: my wife having our kids and being told wife and children were doing well

-BUDDY HACKETT
Comedian/Actor, It's a Mad, Mad, Mad, Mad World, The Rifleman

I've had several best days: the day I got married, the birth of my first son, Philip – in fact the birth of all my seven sons – and now the birth of my first grandson.

-JOSEPH CAMPANELLA

Actor; Silent Running, Ben, Mannix, The Colbys, The Bold Ones: The Lawyers

The day I was born… No cares! I'm still the happiest guy I ever met!

-MOREY AMSTERDAM

Actor/Comedian, Murder, Inc., Beach Party, When Nature Calls, The Dick Van Dyke Show

It would be difficult to decide in my roller coaster existence, just when I had my best day. Perhaps it was the day I married my present wife, Vera. The days of my three children were born. Certainly, the day I came away cancer free from a prostate operation stands near the top. For now, every day seems as if it should be the best of days.

-ROBERT GOULET

Actor/Singer, Honeymoon Hotel, Beetlejuice, Naked Gun, Camelot,
Toy Story 2

Every day is my best day.

-DYAN CANNON
*Actress; Heaven Can Wait, Bob and Carol and Ted and Alice, The Last of
Sheila, Honeysuckle Rose*

Being on stage making 1500 people laugh your socks off!

-BERNARD FOX
Actor; Bewitched, Titanic, The Mummy

Everything becomes possible from my birthday.

-RUBY DEE
Actress; A Raisin In The Sun, Edge of the City, The Jackie Robinson Story, Do the Right Thing

Every day is the best day for me.

-ESTELLE HARRIS

Actress; Stand and Deliver, Out to Sea, Odd Couple II, Toy Story, Seinfeld, Suite Life of Zack and Cody

My wedding day, marrying Sacha Baron Cohen in Paris, in a small traditional Jewish ceremony. My husband (Sacha Baron Cohen) wanted no fuss-just us.

-ISLA FISCHER

Actress; Wedding Crashers, Confessions of a Shopaholic, The Great Gatsby, Now you See Me

My Best Day was the day I opened the school (Oprah Winfrey's Leadership Academy School for Girls, Johannesburg, Africa) for those girls. The next best day coming up will be the day they graduate.

-OPRAH WINFREY

Actress / Producer / Talk Show Host; The Color of Purple, The Women of Brewster Place, The Butler, Selma, The Oprah Winfrey Show

Getting Lost in Space was my Best Day, although I have done other work, but I loved that series

-BILLY MUMY

Actor; Lost in Space, Babylon 5, Space Cases, Twilight Zone

Professionally "10" for the doors it opened and personally any day with my family is a blessed day

-BO DEREK
Actress; Bolero, 10, Tommy Boy

Any day I am hanging out with my three kids.

-BILLY BOB THORNTON

Actor; Fargo, Bad Santa, Tombstone, Sling Blade

My greatest day was when I met my present husband.

-VERA RALSTON

Actress; I, Jane Doe, Dakota, The Fighting Kentuckian, Thunder Across the Pacific

When (Steven) Sondheim announced that-though there were better singers-my voice, look, and personality won me the role in "*Sweeny Todd*", it was probably the best day of my life.

-HELENA BONHAM CARTER

Actress; The King's Speech, Mary Shelley's Frankenstein, Harry Potter Series, Sweeny Todd. Ocean's 8

My 'Best Day'? Too many Best Days, too numerous to mention--& all of them personal with my husband and children.

-ANNE MEARA

Actress; The Boys From Brazil, National Museum, The Out-of-Towners, Zoolander

I did a pajama dance for my Birthday, and I danced all night long. My sister surprised me with New Edition serenading me. I had not experienced joy like that since I was a kid. It was the best moment of my entire life.

-RASHIDA JONES

Actress; Cuban Fury, Parks & Recreation, I Love You, Man

Every day is great!

-BURT WARD

Actor; Batman Series, High School U.S.A., Fire in the Night, Starquest

Today is my Best Day! Make the best of each day.

-ADAM WEST

Actor; Batman series, Robinson Crusoe on Mars, FBI Story, Tammy and the Doctor, The Fairly OddParents

Getting my SAG card-it meant so much to me. I enjoyed WKRP (in Cincinnati) so much; it was a dream come true.

-TIM REID

Actor; Richard Pryor Show, Snoops, Mother Juggs & Speed.

Aside from my family and children, and basking in their success, my best day was the luck of being so fortunate to land "*Growing Pains*". Another thrill was being inducted into the Canadian Walk of Fame.

-ALAN THICKE

Actor; Raising Helena, The Alan Thicke Show, Burkes Law, Growing Pains

Although I am known as "Alice Mitchell" from Dennis the Menace –my earlier career in movies like "*Mr. & Mrs. North*", "*The Tin Man*" and others were pure joy on the set.

-GLORIA HENRY

Actress; Racing Luck, Riders in the Sky, The Tougher They Come, Dennis the Menace

My best day was Dennis the Menace-the best job ever; day in and day out.

-JAY NORTH

Actor; Queen for a Day, The George Goble Show, Colt .45, Dennis the Menace

My best role was filming "*Roots*". The miniseries was a blessing and such a breakthrough. I was fortunate to continue to work after that…some of my brothers & sisters were not so fortunate. But it was a powerful message and I loved playing Fiddler.

Getting the Best Supporting Actor for "An Officer and a Gentleman" was the highlight and Best Day of my rich and prolific career. I went into the Oscar ceremony in a relaxed frame of mind. Here comes Christopher Reeve and Susan Sarandon, they mentioned my name and I thought I was dreaming. Then my agent said, "Get up there"

-LOUIS GOSSETT JR
Actor; A Raisin in the Sun, The Choirboys, An Officer and a Gentleman, Iron Eagle Series, Roots,

F*#@ing every day! Life is the best!

-LORI PETTY

Actress; Tank Girl, Point Break, A League of Their Own

I believe anyone who has lived through World War II must consider their best day to be THE END OF THAT WAR!

Good luck on your book and congratulate yourself on your survival

-JUDD HIRSCH

Actor; Ordinary People, Independence Day, Man on the Moon, Numbers, Taxi, Dear John

I am not going to have a better day, a more magical moment, than the first time I heard my daughter giggle.

-SEAN PENN

Actor; Mystic River, Gangster Squad, I am Sam. Milk, Taps

My best day was today!

-BEAU BRIDGES

Actor; The Fabulous Baker Boys, P.T. Barnum, My Name is Earl

Tomorrow- I presume!

-DAWN WELLS

Actress; Gilligan's Island, Palm Springs Weekend, High School USA

1. Graduated Girard College Philadelphia, PA January 30, 1942
2. Commissioned 2nd Lt U.S. Army Air Corps January 15, 1944
3. Returned to United States after 44 combat Missions-August 1, 1945 in New Guinea and Philippines
4. Birth of my son David April 3, 1955
5. Birth of my daughter Kimberly September 5, 1957

Today & tomorrow and so on.

-RUSSELL JOHNSON
Actor; Tumbleweed,, The Californians, The Silent, Twilight Zone, Gilligan's Island

My Best Day is every day I wake up with someone to love and something to do!

-ARLENE DAHL

Actress, My Wild Irish Rose, A Southern Yankee, Ambush, The Diamond King, Land Raiders

My best day was when we were on Big Thunder Mountain and he (my husband to be; Josh Dallas) said, "This is the best day of my life". I was like, we are totally getting married"

-GINNFER GOODWIN

Actress; Big Love, Zootopia, Walk the Line, A Single Man, Once Upon a Time

We had always planned to have about six children, Michael and me. Yet we had only one beautiful daughter, an actress. My grandson is 16. Motherhood means everything to me. The whole family getting together—it's the best day you could have.

-DAME JUDY DENCH

Actress; James Bond Series: Golden Eye, A Room with a View, Henry V, Tea with Mussolini

My best day was meeting Mother Theresa in person! True!!

-KAYE BALLARD

Actress; The Ritz, Gypsies, The Mother's in Law, Modern Love

My Best Day is today!

-JULIE ADAMS

Actress; Bend of the River, The Swamp Thing, Wings of Hawks, Horizon West

Being in the *Longest Yard* as an actor was my best day.

-JOE KAPP

Professional Football Player/Actor; The Longest Yard

Fortunately, I have enjoyed; and continue to enjoy an extraordinary life of many wonderful and memorial days. And, as in any life, there have been some very trying times. Some bad days, but you go on, as you have, Mark.

However, to say that a particular day was my "best" seems, to me, to suggest: that's it, there have been and will be no more." I look forward to every day, with its particular plans, schedules, and unknowns, as a good day.

I have been blessed with a great gift in my wife, Klaire. We continue to pursue and enjoy a vigorous, meaningful life. We work at it: staying healthy, stay vertical, enjoy & pay attention to life.

But, if asked as an actor, my Broadway debut in "Irene" in 1973 was my Best Day. It was my first taste of the joy of acting, and I won the "Theatre World Award" for my role.

I look forward to many, many more Best Days, and why not?

-MONTE MARKHAM
Actor; Project X, Airport 77, Neon City, The Guns of the Magnificent Seven

I started out acting a bit late in life, so my best day was landing my first part. I was in "*Johnny Mnemonic*" and it was amazing. Life is beautiful-every day is my best day.

-DINA MEYERS

Actress; Dragon Hart, Bats, Star Trek; Nemesis; Starship Troopers

Aside from having my two amazing kids, I love this business. I was very lucky to land the breakout role in "*The Blue Lagoon*". It was magical and led to Dallas…and so many other roles.

-CHRISTOPHER ATKINS

Actor; A Night in Heaven, Swan Lake, Blue Lagoon, Dead Man's Island

My life has been a best day-getting to act alongside my beautiful mother (Barbara Hale) is definitely a best day. I had a blast with Bill Culp on The Greatest American Hero, and so many more it is too hard to focus on one.

-WILLIAM KATT

Actor; House, Search of the Lost Legend, Big Wednesday, Butch and Sundance: The Early Years. Carrie, Greatest American Hero

Marrying my wife, Amy, was the best decision of my life. I look back fondly on my life & films and cannot single out one best moment. I have to say that "*Fast Times at Ridgemont High*" was a blast—a great cast & who knew how well everyone's careers would have taken off?

-JUDGE REINHOLTZ

Actor; Ruthless People, Beverly Hills Cop ,The Santa Clause, Fast Times at Ridgemont High

Being able to work with my brother on "*My Three Sons*" was a highlight in my life.

-BARRY LIVINGSTON

Actor; Maters of the Universe, Jersey Boys, Sidewinders, Argo, War Dogs, My Three Sons

My Best Day was the day my daughter, Samantha was born.
She's the best!

-STANLEY LIVINGSTON
*Actor; Errand Boy, Attack of the 60 foot Centerfold, How the West Was Won,
Rally 'Round the Flag, Boys, My Three Sons,*

My perfect day is with Calista, the kids, whichever one is available, the little bit of work, little bit of play-good food, great glass of wine and a good sleep.

-HARRISON FORD

Actor; Air Force One, Indiana Jones Series, Star Wars, Presumed Innocent, Witness, Patriot Games

When I lay in bed, when I wake up and I realize that I am awake with my arms in the air: I will have a good day, and excellent day.

-ERNEST BORGNINE

Actor; The Wild Bunch, Marty, From Here to Eternity, McHale's Navy, Airwolf

The older I get, the more I realize what a blessing it is just to be alive. My Best Day is yet to come. They have all been good so far.

-JOE MANTEGNA

Actor / Producer; Glengarry Glen Ross, Money Pit, Godfather III, The Last Hit Man, Forget Paris, Criminal Minds

All of 'em…My best days have been every one that led up to today which is one of my best days also.

-ARTE JOHNSON

Actor / Comedian; Laugh in, Love at First Bite

I have been lucky enough to have many, many "Best Days" so it would be hard for me to isolate a particular one, I have been gifted with a wonderful family, career, friends, and, thank heaven, good health.

-BARBARA RUSH
Actress; Peyton Place, Sins & Sinners, The Seekers, Hombre, Robin and the 7 Hoods

At my age, I have been married 65 years to the same wonderful woman, with 4 grown and healthy sons, 7 terrific grandkids, answering your question is an exercise in futility.
The Best Day? The day I was born, got married, had our children, celebrated so many wonderful Christmases, Birthday's, etc. Maybe tomorrow will be the best.

-WILLIAM SHALLERT
Actor; Bag of Bones, Mighty Joe Young, The Incredible Shrinking Man, Nancy Drew, Patty Duke Show

The next one.

-DENNIS FARINA

Actor; Get Shorty, Midnight Run, The Mod Squad, Reindeer Games, , Law and Order

Thank you for the note. I've had so many Best Days. It would be hard to single one out. If I did pick out one as an actor, it was being inducted into the Television Hall of Fame. It was an earth-shaking moment. To think I was going to be joining folks like Johnny Carson and Lucille Ball was just incredible. A second highlight was winning an Emmy in 2013 as guest star on "the Big Bang Theory. I consider myself very lucky.

-BOB NEWHART

Actor / Comedian; Hell is for Heroes, Elf, The Bob Newhart Show, The Librarian, Newhart

Life is good-and getting my start in movies made everything else possible. I am grateful.

-RICHARD ROUNDTREE
Actor; Shaft, Roots, Days of the Assassin, Inchon, City Heat

Marrying fellow actor Dondre Whitfield

-SALLI RICHARDSON-WHITFIELD
Actress; I am Legend, Antwone Fischer, Black Dynamite, Soul of the Game

The birth of my three children are all great days

-ROBIN WILLIAMS
Actor; Good Will Hunting, Hook, Good Morning Vietnam, The World According to Garp, Mork & Mindy

A day with my son, Yoby, is a perfect day. I live up on this Cliffside, and recently we walked to the local café and met my dear, dear friends for breakfast with their kids. After, we hiked back up the hill. Then, in the afternoon we went to a friend's house where there were more kids, and we played and swam and ate a yummy dinner and went home and had a bath.

-CONNIE BRITTON
Actress; The Brothers McMullen, Me, Earl, and the Dying Girl, Friday Night Lights, Nashville

In our bed, making our children, and in the hospital, watching them being born were my happiest moments.

-MATT DAMON

Actor; Jason Bourne Series, Good Will Hunting, The Talented Mr. Ripley, The Departed, The Martian

I have had 3 best days:

1) Being in Marnie
2) My wonderful daughter, Melanie
3) My granddaughter, Dakota Johnson

-TIPPI HEDREN
Actress; The Birds, Marnie, Pacific Heights, A Countess in Hong Kong

I am going to cheat on this one. My Best Day. I have been blessed with many good days. At first this sounded like a tough choice, but after a little thought it turns out this is an easy one. As long as I can change the rules to make it my best day times three, that is. Talking about the day my three children; Nick, Mike and Gina were born. No, they were not born on the same day. They were born on different days and years apart. But to me they are all the same day, the same year, the same overwhelming experience. I mean seriously, how could I pick just one of those days over the other. To witness this Miracle on three separate days is powerful stuff. To see your wife, use strength and power that you've never witnessed before. To see this tiny new person for the first time. Who are they and why did they choose us? How is it I love this little plucked chicken instantly and unconditionally? What's going on!? The profound experience of seeing new life come into this world seems to have no rival. Not to me. To fall in love three times over. How lucky can a man get!

That day times three had a pretty big effect on me. And it doesn't end there. Thirty-five years have passed now since that first best day. Those three tiny people are bigger now. They are all doing fine, thank God. Not everything is perfect all the time, but one thing remains true as ever. That one special day in 1976, 1979, and 1984 remains easily

THE BEST DAY EVER

-JOE REGALBUTO
Actor; Murphy Brown, Magnum PI, Street Hawk

Today is the day

-EDD "KOOKIE" BYRNES
Actor; 77 Sunset Strip, The Secret Invasion, Grease, Darby's Rangers

The recent surprise meeting of my childhood crush, Shia LaBeouf, was the best day ever.

-SELENA GOMEZ
Actress; Monte Carlo, Another Cinderella Story, Princess Protection Program, Wizards of Waverly Place

When my book made the NY Times best seller list the same day my son was born. My publisher called to say congratulations. I thought it was for the birth of my son, but it was to tell me my book was on the NY Times best seller list. What are the odds?

-JOHN O'HURLEY
Actor / Host / Author; 7 Days in Vegas, Seinfeld, Loving, To Tell the Truth

I've never been a fan of the good ol' days. For me the Best Day
has always
been this one.

-VALERIE HARPER
*Actress; Freebie and the Bean, Chapter Two, Rhoda, The Mary Tyler Moore
Show, The Hogan Family*

Oliver Stone tested my mettle filming *Any Given Sunday*, having me do the locker room scene in the buff. I knew Oliver was going to see how far he could take things in those locker-room scenes. I know he wanted a real reaction from me, and I was determined not to give it to him. So, on that day I kept both my eyes up and refused to be shocked by anything. But really, it was the best day of my life.

-CAMERION DIAZ

Actress; My Best Friend's Wedding, There's Something About Mary, Charlies Angels, The Mask

My perfect day would begin with my daughter's smile and end
with a nice glass of vino and then go to bed early

-TIFFANI THIESSEN
Actress; Hollywood Ending, White Collar, Saved by The Bell, The Ladies Man

There are too many to count

-CELESTE HOLM
Actress, The Tender Trap, High Society, All About Eve, Gentleman's Agreement, Oklahoma

Dancing with Fred Astaire was my happiest moment in "*The Sky's the Limit*"

-JOAN LESLIE

Actress / Dancer; High Sierra, Sergeant York, Too Young To Know, Yankee Doodle Dandy

My best day was July 17, 1956-it was my first day as a professional comedian. In Chicago at Mister Kelly's on Rush Street. Finally, I would begin to earn a living in the arts.

-SHELLY BERMAN
Comedian/Actor/ Writer; Divorce, American Style, A Family Affair, Rawhide, Meet the Fockers

As you know, I don't ask for much. But can you please tell me: what exactly is a "Best Day"?

For <u>WHO</u>? About <u>WHAT</u>?? And for WHAT PERIOD ??

"<u>BETTER</u>" thank all the ones I have had?? Or am I in competition with some <u>Neighbors</u>, or some <u>Religious Group</u> ???—And, if it's <u>MY</u> "Best Day", wouldn't I have to wait till I'll have <u>HAD</u> all mine???? And doesn't everybody know that SOME people have "Best Days" <u>EVERY</u> Day???...While others on the same block...even the same family...are in intense therapy and on severe medication JUST TO HAVE <u>ONE</u>????

(My mother wouldn't have admitted she ever came <u>NEAR</u> one.)

And what about Warren Beatty & Hugh Hefner who only have Best <u>NIGHTS</u>?? Is a glib <u>6-year-old</u> qualified to answer?? And what "day" is best for some of those <u>Swedes</u> and <u>Norwegians</u> that don't get any??

What about politicians, who don't have <u>TIME</u> for them?? Or SENIORS, who don't <u>REMEMBER</u>? Or CLERGYMEN, who are not <u>SUPPOSED</u> to have 'em???

What would <u>ORSON WELLES</u> say? Or <u>MICHEALANGELO</u>?? Or <u>BELLA LUGOSI</u>?? Or <u>JOHN GOTTI</u>?? Or <u>GROUCHO MARX</u>?? Or <u>THE MARQUEE DE SADE</u>??

-And, after all, doesn't "<u>BEST</u>" reeeally discriminate against "<u>WORST</u>"...for which the ACLU would demand equal time, public reinstatement, and two years back pay???

And what of our <u>Latino</u> brothers, who would, at the very least, expect "BEST" properly <u>asterisked</u>?? -As would our <u>Asian</u> friends, and <u>Arab</u> neighbors – the local <u>French</u> and <u>Italian</u> and <u>Greek, Korean</u> and <u>Vietnamese</u>, the <u>Chads</u> and <u>Bosnians.</u> (North and South)
We wouldn't want to forget the Sight & Hearing Impaired: As well as our Armed Forces serving us all over the globe- (ABSENTEE BALLOTS would be in order).

And what about LYING…<u>LYING?</u>? What are the penalties there ??? (<u>ANYBODY</u> can say "<u>I had 200 Best Days last Thursday</u>" What of that??

And lastly, what about <u>BENJAMIN BEST & JEREMIA DAY</u>, who, last I checked, had the whole thing wrapped up lock, stock and barrel ??? (You'll be in court the rest of your life.) No, I'm afraid you're gonna have to come up with something better than "Best Day"

Best <u>HOTEL</u>? Best <u>RECIPE</u>? Best <u>DENTIST</u>? Best <u>WAR</u>? Best <u>CUMBERBUN?</u>
Best <u>SPINAL TAP</u>? Best <u>BAR MITZVAH</u>? Best <u>BOWEL MOVEMENT</u> ? Best <u>BANKRUPTCY</u>? Best <u>CRIMINAL THOUGHT</u>? Best <u>FIST-FIGHT</u>? Best <u>SCAR</u>? Best <u>TUNA CASSEROLE</u>? …..

PS- My best day is being with my wife, Shirley Jones

-MARTY INGELS
Actor/Comedian; Wild and Wonderful, For Singles Only, I'm Dickens, He's Fester

My best days were when I had my sons. I am an only child, so having kids around me is special. I have 12 grandchildren, and we are all so close, so they are around me all of the time-a dream come true!

-SHIRLEY JONES

Actress/Singer: Carousel, Oklahoma! The Music Man, Elmer Gantry, The Partridge Family,

Watching my son come into the world

-MICHELLE LEE
Actress; Knots Landing, How to Succeed in Business without Really Trying, The Love Bug

Every day I walk on a set is a Best Day; I love this life.

-KEVIN DOBSON
Actor, Klute, Midway; Kojak, Knots Landing

I'm afraid I can't single out one specific "Best Day." Every day I'm completely engaged in something I love is a day that couldn't be any better.
It might be creative writing, singing, a concert, or an intense conversation. Then I feel whole and Happy and The Day Sings! It happens a lot-for which I'm grateful.

-BARBARA FELDON
Actress; Get Smart, Fitzwilly, A Vacation in Hell, East Side/ West Side

It is quite difficult for me to say exactly which day was "My Best Day Ever" as I've been blessed with so many. Chief among them the day I married my beautiful bride Gina, and those days our three wonderful children were born. But certainly, the birth of my first child, our daughter Sydney, would be a pretty hard day to beat. It also spawned what I consider to a fairly humorous moment, which starred my beloved father, actor, Jack Lemmon.

You see, just as Gina was going through the actual final moments of delivery, Pop, with his usual perfect timing, had strutted into the hospital room, where he found Gina yelping, our OBGYN, Ed Liu, yelling "PUSH!" and Lamazing-like mad. I shouted a distraction, "hey Lem," over the curtain and noted a look of horror on Pop's face. Ten minutes later found Gina and me glowing as we looked down at our beautiful Syd, and then there was a realization-where's Pop? Gina looked around, called out, "Pop?" A moan came from around the corner. I went over to investigate and found Pop laying on a gurney, hooked up to oxygen and a blood pressure monitor, Ed Lui waving smelling salts under his nose. Ed looked up at me and said, "You guys did great, wish I could say the same for Jack."

But that being said, I think every day, when I look into the eyes of my beloved children and deep inside see just a little twinkle of the magic they inherited from their grandpa Jack, well then, every day becomes "My Best Day Ever."

-CHRIS LEMMON
Actor / Author; Duets, Thunder in Paradise, Just Before Dawn. Airport '77, That's Life!

My Best Days are being with Felicia and family, playing golf with friends, and making movies- it's Magic Time!

-JACK LEMMON

Actor; Mister Roberts, The Apartment, Some Like it Hot, The Odd Couple, Glengarry, Glen Ross

I've had some really good days and I've had some really bad days. I guess my best day, or best time, was when I realized that I was not as smart as I thought I was, and I was beginning to have some understanding of what this life is all about.

-MORGAN WOODWARD
Actor; Cool Hand Luke, Firecreek, The Life and Legend of Wyatt Earp, Dallas,

First of all, every day and every event that occurs carries within it the chance of being part of one's best day. And almost as soon as you decide that something that happened on your twelfth birthday could never be topped, you remember what happened on your fortieth that was better.

I guess I would start with the first time I felt that I was in love in high school and then meeting my wife almost twenty years later. But neither tops our first baby and then our second. It has also amazed me to realize that I can find even more pleasure in their success than I find in mine. I remember their graduations from college with more clarity and joy than I remember my own. All of those were great days and inseparable, one from the other.
I have in general always been a one foot in front of the other kind of person. I try to maintain my balance in an ever-changing world and business. One day you are the talk of the town, the next, no-one remembers your name. One year you bounce from continent to continent with work and play and two years later you count change to see if you have enough money to drive to the beach for a day. And then the whole cycle repeats itself.

So, my answer is actually kind of ordinary, and I hope down to earth. Tomorrow is my best day, the day that I haven't had yet and who knows what will happen. It begins with waking up. Waking up is always a good sign. Waking up lets you know that the potential of something fine hangs in the air. As I drifted into sleep tonight, I might not think that today was especially significant, but I know that it will lead to tomorrow and who knows, I might wake up again.

-PETER HASKELL
Actor; The Legend of Earl Durand, Mandrake, Ryan's Hope, Rich Man Poor Man II

My Best Days are many. I am very proud of Dalton Trumbo's name on Spartacus' credits for the screen play—under his true name to help break the blacklist. Any day that my wife Anne and I contribute to a new park or school through the Douglas Foundation, and most of all, time with my wonderful family.

-KIRK DOUGLAS

Actor / Author; Detective Story, Lonely are the Brave, Spartacus, Gun Fight at the OK Corral, The Bad and the Beautiful, Ace in the Hole

My Best Day was on the set of "*A League of their Own*" when Jack McDowell coached me, and Charlie Hough pitched to me in Comiskey Park in the bull pen for 30 minutes.

-TRACY REINER

Actress; When Harry Met Sally, Masque of the Red Dawn, Apollo 13, Die Hard, A League of Their Own

I did theater early, it was the steppingstone to my career and of course, meeting and falling in love with Martin (Landeau)

-BARBARA BAIN

Actress; Cinnamon Carter, Mission Impossible, Savage!, Richard Diamond, Private Detective

My entire life is full of Best Days, but if I had to pick one it would have to be two. *North By Northwest* is my classic role that is dear to my heart, and the best cast ever was to be in *Missio*n Impossible...it opened so many doors.

-MARTIN LANDEAU

Actor; North by Northwest, Mission Impossible, Space: 1999, Nevada Smith, Ed Wood, Tucker; the Man and his Dream

Life makes me happy-every day brings me joy and the present day is my Best Day. I have had so many best days, work wise, be my first movie. A small unknown part but it started me on my way to so many opportunities. Working with John Wayne, Robert Wagner, Troy Donahue, and of course, the wonderful Bill Holden has been such a wonderful joy.

-STEPHANIE POWERS

Actress; Mistral's Daughter, Hart to Hart, The Feather and Father Gang, The Boatniks, McClintock!, The Girl from U.N.C.L.E.

ALL DAYS ARE GOOD. I've had a fine life at pretend and enjoyed every moment.

-CLU GULAGAR

Actor; The Tall Man, The Last Picture Story, The Virginian, Winning, The Killers

My Best Day was the day I married my wife, Amy.

-DANNY BONADUCE
Actor/Radio Personality, The Partridge Family, Corvette Summer, Danny!

My best day occurred in 1950, in the evening of my beloved wife's death. She came to me physically twice in a huge embrace that enveloped my entire body and with whispered words in my ear. I can only assume that our blessed Savior was with her, but in any case, she received permission to say farewell.

-EFREM ZIMBALIST JR
Actor; 77 Sunset Strip, The FBI, Maverick, Harlow, Wait Until Dark

The day my son, Jake, was born, I delivered him, and he is 22 years old now.

-ROBERT HAYES

Actor; Airplane, Vanished, Spider-Man, Cat's Eye, Honeymoon Academy, Dt T and the Women

Every morning is a best day. I look Forward to each day.

-JONATHAN WINTERS
Actor / Comedian; It's a Mad, Mad, Mad, Mad, World, The Russians are Coming, The Russians are Coming, Mork & Mindy, The Johnathan Winters Show,

My best day is being with family & filming a movie. It gives me
great joy to complete a film and see it come together.

-GARRY MARSHALL

*Director/ Producer/ Screen Writer / Actor; Pretty Woman, Beaches, The
Princess Diaries, Valentine's Day, New Year's Eve*

I have had a great career and life, but my best day was opening my theater "The Moon River Theater" in Branson, MO, it was a great dream come true.

-ANDY WILLIAMS
Singer/ Actor; Janie, Kansas City Kitty, Something in the Wind, Ladies Man, The Andy Williams Show

It is hard to choose a single Best Day. In my career, getting cast on the great westerns "*Lawman*" & "*Laredo*" and guest casted on Wagon Train, Maverick and others started me on my amazing journey.

-PETER BROWN

Actor; No Time for Sergeants, Attack at Dawn, Fist of Iron, Hell to Pay, Lawman

Being with my family is always a best day. Doing Kojak was another best day, and I was working with my brother, George.

-TELLY SAVALAS

The Young Savage, The Greatest Story Ever Told, The Dirty Dozen, The Scalp Hunters, Kojak

Apart from the obvious recognition from "*Flashdance*", my first role in "*Goodbye, Columbus*" holds a great place in my heart.

-MICHAEL NOURI
Actor, Flashdance, 61*, Black Ice, Brothers and Sisters, Damages, NCIS

M*A*S*H- it was 11 years of best days

-LORETTA SWIT
Actress; Freebie and the Bean, SOB, Hell Have No Fury, M*A*S*H

My Best Day?

Personally, speaking, it was the day I first became a grandfather, an occasion I've had the pleasure of repeating several times since.

Professionally, it was December 11th, 1989, my musical, "City of Angels," opened on Broadway and proved to be a critical, as well as a long-running, success. Only twenty-four hours earlier, on December 10th, my play, "Mastergate," had been forced to close due to its poor box office appeal.

The experience of knowing success and failure over such a short time span went a long way toward teaching me how to deal with both possibilities over a lifetime.

-LARRY GELBART
*Director/ Writer/Screenwriter, M*A*S*H, Tootsie, The Wrong Box, A Funny Thing Happened to Me on the Way to The Forum*

My happiest day was September 1, 1961 when I left the hospital with my new baby boy in my arms.

-ELLEN BURSTYN
Actress; The Last Picture Show, The Exorcist, Sam Time, Next Year

Doing the show, *"Eastbound and Down"*

-MICHAEL PENA
Actor; CHIPs, Ant Man, American Hustle, Gone in 60 Seconds, East Bound and Down

My best day was the day I went with my mother, Sally Kirkland, Sr; my director Yorek Bogayavich and my Spiritual Teacher; John Rogers, to the Oscars in 1988- I was nominated for Best Actress for 1987 film, *Anna*. I was so ecstatic to be in the same category as Meryl Streep, Glenn Close, Cher and Holly Hunter. It was humbling.

-SALLY KIRKLAND
Actress; Going Home, Cinderella Liberty, Anna, Bite the Bullit

Every morning I awaken is My Best Day.

-NANCY KOVACK
*Actress; When Strangers Meet, Diary of a Madman, Jason and the Argonauts,
The Outlaws is Coming, The Silencers*

There is one particular day that will always stand out in my mind. The town I grew up in, Harvey, Illinois, named a street after me. This was so very meaningful to me because I grew up with eight brothers and sisters and we were truly the poorest family in Harvey. I shined shoes in taverns and sold newspapers on the corner. I set pins in bowling alleys and caddied in the summertime. So to...have a street named after me turned out to be quite a special day.

-TOM DREESEN

Comedian/Actor, Space Balls, The Rat Pack, Trouble with the Curve, Columbo, Murder She Wrote

The day I was born.

-EDDIE ALBERT
Actor; The Longest Yard, The Wagons Rolled at Night, Roman Holiday, The Heart Break Kid, Green Acres,

Your request for a comment on "My Best Day" made me think about many of the events in my life and where on a scale of "best" these events and days might reside.

Since I am trying to stay in a state of being, not living in the past, unable to foresee the future; I try to be here; "NOW" in the moment.

So, I guess "My Best Day" is "NOW/TODAY"

-LARRY GELMAN
Actor; Super Dad, Girls Just Want to Have Fun, Mr. Saturday Night

My best days have been the birthdays of my daughters.

-KEN BURNS
Filmmaker; Documentaries: Baseball, The Roosevelts, The Civil War, Jazz, Prohibition

As for me, I don't have a "Best Day"' they are all wonderful and I am 93.

-DON PARDO

Announcer; The Price is Right, Three on a Match, Jeopardy, Saturday Night Live

Walking in the morning in Beverly Hills. Then after an hour and a half sitting in the sunshine in my garden…. getting in my Range Rover to tend to personal errands.

-RICHARD ANDERSON

Actor, The Six Million Dollar Man, The Gun Fight at Dodge City, The Wackiest Ship in the Army

My life has been a great day, but to pick one, it was my first movie (Blue Denim) that started it all.

-ROBERTA SHORE
Actress; Lolita, The Shaggy Dog, Young Savages, The Virginian

My best day was the day I "accepted the Lord" as my personal Savior.

At age 18, I was signed to a long-term movie contract after being "discovered" one morning on my way to High School. I seemed to have the world in my hands-fame, stardom, and on my way to becoming a legendary actress of my time. But I was in an unfamiliar, fast moving lifestyle that I was totally unprepared for. I was insecure and despondent, and when my friend, Marilyn, took her life I cried out to God for help and guidance. He heard my plea, and warmth and love engulfed me.

-RHONDA FLEMING

Actress; Spellbound, Cry Danger, Gunfight at the OK Corral, Out of the Past, Pony Express

The Joy and wonder of being in *"ET, the Extra Terrestrial"* was magical.

-DEE WALLACE STONE
Actress; Cujo, The Howling, ET the Extra Terrestrial, Secret Admirer

August 16, 1985, my dad took me and my brothers Andre and Tony to see the Fresh Fest at the Nassau Coliseum, on Long Island. We saw Whodini, the Fat Boys, and Grandmaster Flash. Greatest Day of my life.

The birth of my children were big days too, but billions of people have children-only 15,000 people saw that show.

-CHRIS ROCK

Actor/ Comedian/ Producer; The Longest Yard, Grown Ups, Saturday Night Live, Everybody hates Chris

My Best Day was the day I married Bobby Troup.

-JULIE LONDON

Actress / Singer; The Fat Man, Saddle the Wind, The Wonderful Country,
Emergency!

Being on Dallas was the best time of my life and my Best Days. My wife would laugh at me because I would go to work earlier than needed every day. I was like a little kid wanting to go and be with my friends and play. Larry Hagman was my best friend, and I love Linda Gray, Victoria Principal, along with all of the cast. I would have done Dallas forever.

Another Best Day was when I turned 21. My parents, as I did with my children, made me and my sister a deal. If we didn't smoke until we were 21, they would buy us a car. I was living in Seattle when I turned 21, and they drove out to surprise me with a red 2968 Camero 327, it was my dream car. I was literally running up the furniture, I was so excited. I've never smoked in my life, so it was a great deal.

-PATRICK DUFFY

Actor; Dallas, Step by Step, The Bold and the Beautiful, Welcome to Sweden

When I was a poor kid growing up in the projects of Brooklyn, I never dreamed I'd have a star on the Hollywood Walk of Fame. Now that I am here, this is the Best Day I have ever had.

-TRACY MORGAN

Actor/ Comedian; Head of State, 30 Rock, Martin

I have played a good guy, a bad guy, and anywhere in between. I don't have a favorite roll, there have been too many. But, for shear excitement and fun, my greatest day filming was on the "Pirates of the Caribbean". I enjoyed myself immensely.

-JONATHAN PRYCE

Actor; Tomorrow Never Dies. Glengarry Glen Ross, Pirates of the Caribbean, The Wife. The Two Popes

I have had so many wonderful days in my life- with my husband and family, with friends, on movie & TV sets, and been blessed to be nominated and won some incredible awards. I do have to say that my best role was not one that was award noted but being in "Fatal Attraction" had the most impact. The storyline was great, Anne Archer was perfect as the innocent wife, and Michael Douglas was amazing as the guilty husband, and I loved playing wild, crazily obsessed Alex! When Tom Hanks (in "Sleepless is Seattle") talked to his son abouts dates, "did you see "Fatal Attraction"? Well, I did, and it scared the shit out of me. It scared the shit out of every man in America" I was so thrilled, what a compliment to have my role talked about in another movie.

I love this business!

-GLENN CLOSE

Actress / Producer; The Big Chill, The Natural, Fatal Attraction, The Wife, Damages

Being recognized around the world as "Hagrid" from the "Harry Potter" series has brought me so much pleasure in my career. I am thankful to J.K. Rowling for her books and being cast in the movies is absolutely My Best Day.

-ROBBIE COLTRANE

Actor; Mona Lisa, Golden Eye, Harry Potter Series, The World is Never Enough, Ocean's Twelve

The fact that people thought enough of what I was trying to do throughout my entire career by immortalizing my hands in concrete at the iconic Chinese Theater is a worth this moment, and one of my Best Days ever. I cannot say how grateful I am.

-CICELY TYSON

Actress, Sounder, Bustin' Loose, Fried Green Tomatoes, Diary of a Mad Black Woman, The Help, Guiding Light

I think it is great they are making another remake of "A Star is Born". I saw myself in my character in that film, and I realized I was destroying my life with alcohol and drugs. I am lucky I had the clarity to change myself, or at 82 years old, I know I would still not be here. "A Star is Born" was the best role, and my Best Days since it gave me many Best Days of my life to enjoy.

-KRIS KRISTOPHERSON

Actor/ Singer; Pat Garrett and Billy the Kid, Alice Doesn't Live Here Anymore, A Star is Born, Payback

I've had a great career with many opportunity and memorable days. The events leading up to my first movie role stands out. I was doing a play, and the producer asked me to dye my hair blonde since I was playing a Russian. Ironically, having blonde hair with dark roots standing out, got me the part on my first movie ever, "*Ruthless People*." I was acting with the amazing Bette Midler, Danny Devito, Helen Slater, and Judge Reinholtz, and I felt blessed. Who would have thought that as an ignorant guy wit a semi-bad dye job, that I could turn it into the launching of my career?

-BILL PULLMAN
Actor; Ruthless People, Independence Day, Sleepless in Seattle, The Sinner

My Best Day is today, as I am writing this letter. I realize that there may be better stories, more inspiration in recalling the past. The past is history, the future a mystery. But I can be sure that today can be my Best Day followed by another Best Day tomorrow, and so on. This is how a lifetime gets built.

-BEN MURPHY

Actor; The Thousand Plane Raid, Code Name-Minus One, The Name of the Game, Alias Smith and Jones, Gemini Man, The Winds of War,

My Best Day? Obviously, as an actor, getting "Happy Days" was a blessing! We are still such a family; everyone is such a good friend and we have so much fun.

-ANSON WILLIAMS

Actor / Singer / Director; Happy Days, I married a Centerfold, LA Law, Sabrina the Teenage Witch

I tried for three years in Los Angeles as an actor without getting one part, no commercial, not one line on a show, NOTHING. Being cast as Don Draper on "*Mad Men*" was the luckiest, Best Day of my career. I loved the character and the show premise, but in my wildest dreams I never thought it would take off like it did. Perseverance paid off!

-JON HAMM

Actor; The A-Team, Bridesmaids, Keeping up with the Jones, Bad Times at the El Royale, Top Gun: Maverick, Mad Men

I recently got my star on the Hollywood Walk of Fame, and it made me reflective. I have had many wonderful moments as an actress, including award nominations, but the ceremony was my Best Day. My "friendemy"- Judy Greer spoke, as well as the very funny Steve Carrell and the amazing Bryan Cranston. To share those wonderful thoughts and emotions with my parents and sisters, it was so emotional. It was an honor and such a special day.

-JENNIFER GARNER

Actress /Producer; 13 going on 30, Valentine's Day, Dallas Buyers Club, Peppermint, Alias,

I cannot choose just one Best Day in my career, I loved all of the characters I portrayed. Acting has been so much fun.

James West was one of my favorite roles, but I embraced all the roles in my 3-television series with equal enthusiasm. When I was doing Hawaiian Eye, I learned to surf in Hawaii and learned to mingle with the Hawaiian population. When I did the Wild, Wild West I learned to do stunts and ended up doing all my own stunts which I enjoyed. When I did Baa Baa Black Sheep Squadron, I learned to fly and became a pilot. Subsequently, every role I had I tried to be as close to what I was portraying as possible.

I've been in the business for 50 years, and I've had a good run. I'm happy with what I have done.

-ROBERT CONRAD
Actor; Palm Springs Weekend, Sudden Death, The Lady in Red, Hawaiian Eye, Wild, Wild West, Baa Baa Black Sheep

I don't know if I can choose one Best Day (after marrying my wife); I have had such a long and varied career. The first show I ever saw was "The Lone Ranger" and I thought, that is what I want to do.

In the sixties, everyone you knew became famous. My flatmate was Terence Stamp. My barber was Vidal Sassoon. David Hockney did the menu in a restaurant I went to. I didn't know anyone unknown who didn't become famous.

The three actors I admire the most are all dead: Humphrey Bogart, Spencer Tracy and the French actor, Jean Gabin. They're all very natural, sort of masculine without being overly macho.

Alfie was the first time I was about the title; the first time I became a star in America. So, accolades wise, that was a best moment.

And now, when I look in the mirror, I see someone who is happy with how he looks, because I was never one of the handsome Hollywood people. And I've had success as I've gotten older, because I am able to play characters. I no longer get the girl, but I get the part!

-MICHAEL CAINE
Actor / Producer /Author; The Man Who Would Be King, A Bridge Too Far, Educating Rita, Cider House Rules, Dirty Rotten Scoundrels. Batman Series, Inception

Movies are always fun to be on set, but my Best time was on Police Woman with Angie Dickenson, Ed Bernard, and Earl Holliman. They were all terrific.

-CHARLES DIERKOP
Actor; Butch Cassidy & the Sundance Kid, The Sting, The Hustler, Police Woman

My first movie, "Wild River" was my Best Day. The magic of Hollywood hit me, and it has never worn off. I was uncredited and worked with the great Elia Kazan; what a great start.

-BRUCE DERN

Actor; The Cowboys, The Great Gatsby, Coming Home, The Hateful Eight, Nebraska, Once Upon a Time in Hollywood

I have had a few memorable days in the business, my first part, my 1st major role, and I have worked with some amazing co-stars like Kevin Costner, Robert De Niro, Gene Hackman, John Travolta, Danny Glover and Mel Gibson to name a few.

But, my Best Days filming was with Peirce Brosnan on "*The Thomas Crown Affair*". He and Dennis Leary were a blast, and my character was smart and independent. Everything about the production, script, and cast was first class. I laughed and had so much fun.

-RENE RUSSO

Actress / Producer; Major League, In the Line of Fire, Get Shorty, The Thomas Crown Affair, Thor

One of my Best Days so far was winning the MTV's Best Actor award last spring. MTV abolished gender-specific categories. It indicated that acting is about the ability to put yourself in someone else's shoes and that doesn't need to be separated into two different categories. Brilliant!

-EMMA WATSON

Actress; Harry Potter Series, The Perks of Being a Wallflower, Beauty and the Beast, Little Women

Meeting my friend, Garry Marshall, was my biggest career break and personally, the Best Day of my life. He called me his "good luck charm", and Garry cast me in every single movie he made. I love that man and miss him every day.

-HECTOR ELIZONDO

Actor; The Taking of Pelham One, Two, Three, American Gigolo, Pretty Woman, The Princess Diaries, Valentine's Day,

Recording a duet with Barbara Streisand on my new album and getting two Grammy nominations for the album.

-SETH MCFARLAND

Actor / Singer / Comedian; Tooth Fairy, Ted, A Million Ways to Die in the West, Sing

Getting my Hollywood Walk of Fame Star was one of my Best
Days ever for me.

-HARRY CONNICK JR

*Singer / Actor / Host; Memphis Belle, Little Man Tate, Independence Day,
Hope Floats, Will & Grace, Harry*

Most people would assume my Best Day would be winning my Academy Award. That was a wonderful achievement and a day I'll cherish.

But meeting and becoming friends with Sidney Poitier was and is my greatest day. I live near him now, and we visit as much as possible. I started to record our conversations, he is so wise, funny and has amazing stories. I cherish his friendship for life.

-DENZEL WASHINGTON

Actor / Director / Producer; Malcolm X, Remember the Titans, Glory, American Gangster, Philadelphia, Fences, St. Elsewhere

One of my recent Best Days was being back on the Islands (Hawaiian) filming "*Jumanji- Back to the Jungle*" I grew up in Hawaii and my family had to leave when I was 13, we couldn't afford the rent. I promised myself that I would never let that happen again. The irony on how successful I have become has not been lost on me. I am so excited to have a Christmas released movie, and it is so appropriate that it was filmed in Hawaii.

-DWAYNE 'THE ROCK' JOHNSON
Actor / Producer; The Scorpion King, The Game Plan, San Andreas, Skyscraper, Jumanji- Welcome to the Jungle, Furious, Ballers

Getting to play Martin Crane on "Fraiser" was my greatest moment, it was a role of a lifetime.

-JOHN MAHONEY

Actor; Moonstruck, Eight Men Out, The Manhattan Project, The American President, Frasier,

My Best Day ever was when I met my future husband, Gian Luca, in Paris at a fashion show. We were just married this year (2017) at his parent's house in Italy. That same day I was nominated for an Academy Award for "The Help"; it doesn't get any better than that.

-JESSICA CHASTAIN

Actress; Jolene, The Help, Zero Dark Thirty, Interstellar, The Martian

Moving to New York in 1954 to try show business was my Best Day. I knew one person, and not very well, who I went to UCLA with back in California. I checked into a flea bag motel and was homesick. I love the rain, and it started to rain. Then I turned on the radio, and the weathercaster said, "Hurricane Carol is about to hit New York"

It was a sign!

I then called my one friend, who had me come live at "The Theater House." I got a part in the play "*Once Upon A Mattress*" and on "*The Gary Moore Show*". I worked back-to-back every day, but it was the start of my career and so much fun. It was delightful.

-CAROL BURNETT

Actress / Comedian / Writer; Pete & Tilly, The Four Seasons, Annie, Noises Off, The Carol Burnett Show

My Best Day was getting the call that I was nominated for my first Academy Award. I was so excited! I called me mam, she is my best friend. I never expected it and will never forget the thrill.

-SAOIRSE RONAN
Actress; The Lovely Bones, Lady Bird, Mary, Queen of Scots, Little Woman

Meeting, falling in love with, and marrying my best friend, Rodney Peete was the greatest, Best Day of my life. My family is my life and I cherish them.

-HOLLY ROBINSON-PEETE

Actress; Speed Dating, 21 Jump Street, Hanging with Mr. Cooper, Morning Show Mystery Series

I have had a few struggles in my life, but the blessings have far outweighed any hardships. My family is the world to me.

My music career has always been important to me and opened so many doors. I love to perform.

But, the happiest day for me so far was getting the part on "*NCIS-LA*" on so many levels. It meant so much to me. I switched from rap to mainstream acting. I have a stable job with hours to suit my family. I work with an amazing cast on the best show. I am blessed.

-L.L. COOL J

Rapper/Actor; OZ, Any Given Sunday, Charlie's Angels, S.W.A,T., NCIS Los Angeles, Lip Sync Battle

To start my career, my Best Day was getting the last spot in a drama school. At the bottom of the letter, it said to bring a check for $3,500 the first day. I had just finished college, I was like, I can't ask my dad for more money. I put the letter in the bin, and I was like, that's it; no more acting. The next day I got a bequeath for $3,500 from my grandmother who had died three months before. I was able to go after all.

But my Best Day ever was meeting my wife, Deborra-Lee Furness on an Australian TV Series called *"Correlli"*. Dee is the foundation of our family and therefore my life.

-HUGH JACKMAN

Actor / Singer / Producer; Kate & Leopold, Les Misérables, The Greatest Showman, X-Men, Wolverine

Accepting my father's (Henry Fonda) Academy Award for "On Golden Pond" just five months before his death at the age of 77 was my Best Day. It was the highlight of my career- more so than winning Oscars for "Klute" in 1971 and "Coming Home" in 1978. It was a dream come true.

-JANE FONDA

Actress; Electric Horseman, Klute, Cat Ballou, Barefoot in the Park, Fun with Dick and Jane, TV's Frankie and Grace

I've had many career Best Days, many high points over the years. I look back before I started my three years goodbye tour.

America gave me my start, so I am starting and ending my concerts here in America, I am so grateful.

My touch tone song since 1970 is "*Your Song*"- still singing it makes me grateful.

I went with my gut to agree to do "*The Lion King*"; it opened up new opportunities and gave me new and wonderful fans. It was one of the best decisions of my life.

But my Best Day ever was when David and I had our two kids. Our boys are 5 and 7 right now and bring us such joy. This farewell tour is my thank you to the fans before we focus on our kids. I became a dad later in life, and I love it.

-SIR ELTON JOHN
Singer / Composer / Pianist; Lion King, Rocketman

I have been very lucky to have success in my career, and I have had my share of Best Days. Being on "The New Adventures of the Old Christine" with Julia-Louis Dreyfus and the rest of the cast was amazing. I am about to do a film with Pierce Brosnan, Guy Pierce, and Maya Rudolph this summer (2018), and I am really excited. But my Best Day recently was directing an episode of my show, "Marvel, Agents of S.H.I.E.L.D." for the first time. It was epic!

-CLARK GREGG

Actor / Director; Clear and Present Danger, Iron Man, Mr. Poppers Penguins, Captain Marvel, The New Adventures of the old Christine, Agents of S.H.I.E.L.D

Today (January 2018) is my first Oscar nomination and its my Best Day. This is a dream of a lifetime; I am so excited. Five of my friends flew to NYC for the announcements of the nominations, and I was so nervous. Even after winning a Golden Globe and SAG award for my role in "I, Tanya" I didn't know if I would be nominated or not? I am so thrilled.

-ALLISON JANNEY

Actress; Primary Colors, Hairspray, The Help, The Girl on the Train, I, Tanya, The West Wing, Mom

I have had too many high points in my career to pick just one. My Best Day in acting were the times I have been privileged to perform alongside my father, Robert Alda.

-ALAN ALDA

Actor / Director / Author; Same Time, Next Year; The Four Seasons, Bridge of Spies, The Aviator, M*A*S*H, The Blacklist, Ray Donovan

I am speechless to be the first African American to win the best actor Golden Globe Award for a TV Drama. Today is my best day. "This is Us" series creator, Dan Fogelman, wrote the role that could only be played by a black man. So, it is much harder to dismiss me or anyone who looks like me. I am grateful and honored for the recognition.

-STERLING K. BROWN

Actor; Whiskey Tango Foxtrot, Black Panther, Rise, Supernatural, This is Us,

Getting the lead role in "The Black Panther" has been my Best Day in my career. It has taken a life of its own. Growing up, I did not have a black superhero to look to for confidence. To see kids dressed up like my character, it has important impact and the characters have substances as role models.

-CHADWICK BOSEMAN
Actor, 42, Get on It, Marshall, Captain America: Civil War, Black Panther

I don't know how I have been so lucky in my career; I have spent 9 years each on two great shows and both roles are my best, greatest days as an actress. I came to Los Angeles with no car, no agent, no manager and one commercial reel for auditions. I landed "Everybody Loves Raymond" and then was cast in "The Middle"' both wonderfully written shows with great casts, I love my life.

-PATRICIA HEATON

Actress: Room for Two, Everybody Loves Raymond, The Middle, Carol's Second Act

The birth of our son, Bobby, has been my Best Day. He had successful heart surgery a few months after he was born (2018) and has one more to go. But, thankfully, he is doing well and will continue to do well. My wife and I cherish him every single moment.

-JIMMY KIMMELL

Talk Show Host; Pitch Perfect, Ted, Jimmy Kimmel Live! Prime Time Emmy Host 2012, 2016, 89th Academy Award Host

Oh my! Today is my Best Day, it is the greatest. Hearing my name announced for an Oscar was like getting hit in the head with a baseball bat. Then I began to breath and wonder if I was dreaming or not? This is the best feeling and I am so proud.

-JORDAN PEELE

Actor / Writer / Director; Get Out, US, Wendell and Wild, Key & Peele, The Last O.G., The Twilight Zone

Winning the Best Director Oscar Award in 2010 as the first female director was the best, just the Best Day ever!

-KATHERINE BIGALOW

Director / Producer / Screenwriter; Near Dawn, Point Break, The Hurt Locker, Zero Dark Thirty, Detroit

Being in the film industry and making memories is full of best days. To chose one, being in a James Bond movie. *The Man with the Golden Gun,* was one of my Best Days.

-MARC LAWRENCE

Actor / Author; G Men, The Oxbow Incident, Key Largo, The Asphalt Jungle, The Big Easy

About the Author:

Mark Keys is a Southern California native, residing in Costa Mesa with his wife Laurie, daughters, Page and Megan, their dog, Fumble, and five cats, Lucy, Ethel, Sammy, Frank & Jack-Jack. Mark loves that his mom still lives at the beach in Newport in the house he grew up in, and he spends a lot of time there with her & the girls; and loves walking the beach. He played basketball growing up, in High School, and beyond; as well as body surfed until he injured his back. Mark is an avid reader, enjoys watching classic movies & westerns, collecting film and sports memorabilia, walking and listening to Jazz, Motown, and Rat Pack music. He also loves to travel and going to sporting events & team practices; when health permits. In spite of his numerous surgeries, including 6 back, 1 elbow (Tommy John Surgery) 15 ankle, 3 neck, 4 shoulder, and 11 knee surgeries (plus 4 knee replacements). He also experienced shingles, pneumonia, prostate infection, cancer, MRSA Staph infection. He lost his thyroid, testosterone and does not have an immune system. Mark fights continuous migraines and other health issues every day. But, through all of this, he keeps a positive attitude and outlook to make each day, his best day.

Made in the USA
Middletown, DE
07 January 2023

18953024R00146